Encouraging Words

32-Day Devotional with a bonus day
and a bonus word

DARRYL G. STANTON

*eBooks2go, Inc.
1827 Walden Office Square, Suite 260,
Schaumburg, IL 60173
www.ebooks2go.net
Phone: (847) 598-1150*

© *2020 Darryl G. Stanton. All rights reserved.*

No part of this book may be reproduced, stored in a retrieval system, or transmitted by any means without the written permission of the author.

Published by eBooks2go, Inc.

*ISBN: 978-1-5457-5376-7 (sc)
ISBN: 978-1-6655-0015-9 (e)*

Print information available on the last page.

*Any people depicted in stock imagery provided by Getty Images are models, and such images are being used for illustrative purposes only.
Certain stock imagery* © *Getty Images.*

Scripture quotations marked NKJV are taken from the New King James Version. Copyright © *1982 by Thomas Nelson, Inc. Used by permission. All rights reserved.*

Scripture quotations marked NIV are taken from the Holy Bible, New International Version®. NIV®. Copyright © *1973, 1978, 1984 by International Bible Society. Used by permission of Zondervan. All rights reserved. [Biblica]*

Scripture quotations marked KJV are from the Holy Bible, King James Version (Authorized Version). First published in 1611. Quoted from the KJV Classic Reference Bible, Copyright © *1983 by The Zondervan Corporation.*

This book is printed on acid-free paper.

Because of the dynamic nature of the Internet, any web addresses or links contained in this book may have changed since publication and may no longer be valid. The views expressed in this work are solely those of the author and do not necessarily reflect the views of the publisher, and the publisher hereby disclaims any responsibility for them.

Foreword

Darryl Stanton is a man among men. Few men I've known have been through more hardships spiritually, financially, and physically than him. And yet he still stands. By the grace of his merciful and loving God, he stands.

I had the privilege of walking with Darryl and Jana through his second round of cancer. He never complained. He never even spoke about it, except to say that it was a platform he was going to use to glorify God. I'll never forget the day when Darryl came to church after being healed completely by Jesus from his cancer death sentence. I asked him to stand up and say something. He did… but he never mentioned being healed! All he could do was give glory to God and invite anyone who didn't know his Lord to come to Him now. What a testimony!

Darryl and his queen, Jana, are amazing people who love Jesus and each other with all of their hearts, souls, minds, and strength. I wholeheartedly recommend these scriptures and this journal of Darryl's life with cancer as a testimony to God's faithfulness, and as encouragement from the holy scriptures for anyone who might be going down that same road.

In Christ,
Pastor Colin Conner

Acknowledgment

Dear Melvin and Tumininu Jordan,

I appreciate you and your queen for all the assistance you guys have given me with this book, and for helping me with all the word definitions. I am grateful for both of you. I thank God for you.

With love,
Darryl

Mathew 6:13 NKJV
"And do not lead us into temptation. But deliver us from the evil one. For yours is the kingdom and the power and the glory, forever. Amen."

Mark 16:20 NKJV
"And they went out and preached everywhere, the Lord working with them and confirming the word through the accompanying signs. Amen."

Matthew 28:20 NKJV
"Teaching them to observe all things that I have commanded you; and lo, I am with you always, even to the end of the age. Amen."

Throughout the Bible, Jesus continually taught his disciples how to pray, and how to use Amen at the end of scripture, which means, *so be it*. So today, let your answer to be *Amen*, to what God wants you to do.

Bless

Matthew 5:44 NKJV
"But I say to you, love your enemies, bless those who curse you, do good to those who hate you, and pray for those who spitefully use you and persecute you."

Luke 6:28 NKJV
"Bless those who curse you, and pray for those who spitefully use you."

Romans 12:14 NKJV
"Bless those who persecute you. Bless and do not curse."

The word *bless* also means *to show favor*. When is the last time you blessed those who spitefully used you. Although it is not the easiest thing to do, it is one of the biggest characteristics of Christ. Let today be a day that we bless others. Not just those who deserve it, but also those who do not deserve it.

Courage

Joshua 1:9 NKJV
"Have I not commanded you? Be strong and of good courage; do not be afraid, nor be dismayed, for the Lord your God is with you wherever you go."

Psalms 31:24 NKJV
"Be of good courage, and He shall strengthen your heart, all you who hope in the Lord."

Psalms 27:14 NKJV
"Wait on the Lord; be of good courage, and he shall strengthen your heart. Wait, I say, on the Lord!"

Being of good courage is one of the things that the Lord cannot stress enough. The reason is because, through the trials and seasons of this life, we tend to get stressed, anxious, or discouraged, and God is saying do not lose your courage in the midst. Today, let us practice being of good courage in all seasons of this life.

Destiny

Jeremiah 1:5 NKJV
"Before I formed you in the womb, I knew you. Before you were born, I set you apart; I appointed you as a prophet to the nations."

1 Peter 2:8–9 NIV
"A stone causes people to stumble, and a rock makes them fall. They stumble because they disobey the message, which is also what they were destined for. But you are a chosen people, a royal priesthood, a holy nation, Gods special possession, that you may declare the praises of Him who called you out of darkness into His wonderful light."

1 Corinthians 2:9 NIV
"However, as it is written: no eye has seen, no ear has heard, and no human mind has conceived the things God has prepared for those who love Him."

There is a predetermined destiny for those that love and serve Christ, and there is a destiny for those that do not. Today, as we begin to be sensitive and obedient to God's voice, with every step, we will become closer to our destiny in Christ Jesus.

Encouragement

Matthew 11:28 NKJV
"Come to me, all who are labored and heavy laden, and I will give you rest.

Philippians 1:6 NIV
"…being confident of this, that He who began a good work in you will carry it onto completion until the day of Jesus Christ."

Mark 10:27 NIV
"Jesus looked at them and said, "With man this is impossible, but not with God; all things are possible with God."

God brings encouragement in different ways. Whether you are carrying too much, or people have given up on you, or if you have not received a healing in a long time, remember that what God starts, he will finish. Thank you, Jesus that with Him all things are possible.

Friends

Proverbs 18:24 NKJV
"A man who has friends must also himself be friendly, but there is a friend that sticks closer than a brother."

James 2:23 NKJV
And the scripture was fulfilled which says, "Abraham believed God, and it was accounted to him for righteousness. And he was called the friend of God."

John 15:13 NKJV
"Greater love has no one than this, than to lay down one's life for his friends."

Christ is a friend like no other. He will never leave you nor forsake you, and He is always listening. Today, let's focus on spending more time with our Lord and Savior Jesus Christ in prayer, knowing that He is always listening.

Glory

1 Timothy 1:17 NKJV
"Now to the King eternal, immortal, invisible, to God who alone is wise, be honor and glory, forever and ever. Amen."

2 Timothy 4:18 NKJV
"And the Lord will deliver me from every evil work and preserve me for His heavenly kingdom. To Him be the glory, forever and ever."

Philippians 4:20 NKJV
"Now to our God and Father be glory forever and ever. Amen."

Glory is another way of saying *praise to the Lord*. Glory and praise was never meant for man to take, but unto God be the Glory and Praise. So today, let's make sure that God is getting all the Glory in our walk with Him. Amen.

God

2 John 1:3 NKJV
"Grace, mercy, and peace will be with you from God the Father and from the Lord Jesus Christ, the Son of the Father, in truth and love."

2 Peter 1:17 NKJV
"For He received, from God the Father, honor and glory when such a voice came to Him from Excellent Glory: "This is me, beloved son, in whom I am well pleased."

Titus 1:4 NKJV
"To Titus, a true son in our common faith: grace, mercy, and peace from God the Father and the Lord Jesus Christ, our Savior."

God is a key figure in the three circle. The Son and the Holy Spirit work as one. But God is the Father. We have the privilege to pray to and have a relationship with all three. Today, lets be specific in our prayers and watch our relationship with God the Father grow.

In the name of Jesus, Amen.

Ephesians 5:27 NKJV
"That He might present her to Himself a glorious Church, not having spot or wrinkle or any such thing, but that she should be holy and without blemish."

Ephesians 1:4 NKJV
"Just as He chose us in Him before the foundation of the world, that we should be holy and without blame before Him in love."

Romans 12:1 NKJV
"I beseech you therefore, brethren, by the mercies of God, that you present your bodies a living sacrifice, holy, acceptable to God, which is your reasonable service."

In the word of God, *Holy* means *set apart to God*. Most Christians don't know that God delights in us being separated unto Christ, but the Bible emphasizes this. So today, in prayer, let us examine ourselves to make sure that we are set apart unto Christ.

Instruction

Proverbs 1:7 NKJV
"The fear of the Lord is the beginning of knowledge, but fools despise wisdom and instruction."

Proverbs 4:1 NKJV
"Hear, my children, the instruction of a father, and give attention to know understanding."

Proverbs 10:17 NKJV
"He who keeps instruction is in the way of life, but he who refuses correction goes astray."

Instruction is needed in the life of a man or woman of God. Within the Bible lies our instructions, and it is a privilege for a man or woman of God to know that the Lord of heaven and the earth loves us enough to give us instructions to abide by. Today, let's strive to be sensitive to the voice of God, and listen to the instructions God gives you?

Jesus

Colossians 3:17 NKJV
"And whatever you do in word or deed, do all in the name of the Lord Jesus, giving thanks to God the Father through Him."

Philippians 2:10 NKJV
"That at the name of Jesus every knee should bow, of those in heaven, and of those on earth, and of those under the earth."

1 John 3:23 NKJV
"And this is His commandment: that we should believe on the name of His Son, Jesus Christ, and love one another, as He gave us commandment."

All things that we do as Christians should be in the name of Jesus Christ. There is power in the Name of Jesus. By His name, and His name only. Whatever we do in the Name of Jesus, as His children, we have power.

Kindness

Colossians 3:12 NKJV
"Therefore, as the elect of God, holy and beloved, put on tender mercies, kindness, humility, meekness, long-suffering."

Galatians 5:22 NKJV
"But the fruit of the spirit is love, joy, peace, long-suffering, kindness, goodness, faithfulness."

Proverbs 31:26 NKJV
"She opens her mouth with wisdom, and on her tongue is the law of kindness."

What is rarely seen in schools, homes, relationships, marriages, or churches today is kindness. It is truly the fruit of the spirit, and it is a selfless thing to do. Today, let's exercise the fruit of kindness. You never know who can see God in you by just showing kindness.

Long-suffering

1 Corinthians 6:6 KJV
"By pureness, by knowledge, by long-suffering, by kindness, by the Holy Ghost, by love unfeigned."

Galatians 5:22 KJV
"But the fruit of the spirit is love, joy, peace, long-suffering, gentleness, goodness, faith."

2 Timothy 3:10 NKJV
"But you have carefully followed my doctrine, manner of life, purpose, faith, long-suffering, love, perseverance."

Long-suffering is patiently enduring lasting offense or hardship. So it's something we should imitate every day for others. Christ will not give up on you, so don't give up on others.

Love

Psalms 52:3 NKJV
"You love evil more than good, lying rather than speaking righteousness. Selah."

Matthew 5:44 NKJV
"But I say to you, love your enemies, bless those who curse you, do good to those who hate you, and pray for those who spitefully use you and persecute you."

Romans 5:8 NKJV
"But God demonstrates His own love toward us, in that while we were still sinners, Christ died for us."

Love is an action word (John 3:16), and not what this world displays as love. God not only gives a real description of Love, but He shows it. Today, let's show our love for God in deeds, not just words. Amen.

Marriage

Proverbs 31:10 NIV
"A wife of noble character, who can find? She is worth far more than rubies."

Mark 10:9 NIV
"Therefore, what God has joined together, let no one separate."

Genesis 2:24 NIV
"That is why a man leaves his father and mother and is united to his wife, and they become one flesh."

From the beginning, God ordained marriage to be a blessing. Through His scriptures, He describes the church as His wife, and Himself as the husband. Today, treasure marriage as God would have us to do. Amen.

Motivation

Philippians 4:13 NIV
"I can do all things through Him who gives me strength."

Proverbs 3:5 NIV
"Trust in the Lord with all your heart, and lean not on your own understanding."

Isaiah 41:10 NIV
"So do not fear, for I am with you; do not be dismayed, for I am your God. I will strengthen you and help you; I will uphold you with my righteous right hand."

Throughout the Bible, Christ provides motivation to believe in Him for all things, and to trust that He will always be there for us. Thank you, Jesus. Today, let's have the courage to do His will.

Neighbor

Mark 12:31

Luke 6:35

Ephesians 4:2

"I will love my neighbor as I love myself."

—NIV Bible Study

Noble

Luke 8:15 NKJV
"But the ones that fell on good ground are those who, having heard the word with a noble and good heart, keep it and bear fruit with patience."

Philippians 4:8 NKJV
"Finally, brethren, whatever things are true, whatever things are noble, whatever things are just, whatever things are pure, whatever things are lovely, whatever things are of good report, if there is any virtue and if there is anything praiseworthy—meditate on these things."

Proverbs 18:10 NKJV
"The Name of the Lord is a strong tower; the righteous run to it and are safe."

Noble is another word for *righteousness*. Can people around you say that you are noble? That you are noble at work? That you are noble at home? Today, let us strive to be noble in all that we do, to glorify our Father in heaven.

Obedience

Philippians 2:8 NKJV
"And being found in appearance as a man, He humbled Himself and became obedient to the point of death, even the death of the cross."

Hebrews 5:8 NKJV
"Though He was a Son, yet He learned obedience by the things which He suffered."

Job 36:11 NKJV
"If they obey and serve Him, they shall spend their days in prosperity, and their years in pleasure."

Obedience shows God that you love, trust, and respect Him as the God He is. Obedience touches God's heart.

Passion

1 Corinthians 7:9 NKJV
"But if they cannot exercise self-control, let them marry. For it is better to marry than to burn with passion."

1 Thessalonians 4:5 NKJV
"Not in passion of lust, like the Gentiles who do not know God."

Colossians 3:5 NKJV
"Therefore, put to death your members which are on the earth: fornication, uncleanness, passion, evil desire, and covetousness, which is idolatry."

Passion is something that God does not long for us to have, unless it is for His house or the things of God. Today, let us practice self-control, and only a passion for the things of God. Amen.

Praise

Psalm 113:2

Peter 4:16

Psalm 147:1

"I will praise our God with the fruits of my lips."

—NIV Study Bible.

Power

2 Timothy 1:7 NKJV
"For God has not given us the spirit of fear, but of power, and of love, and of sound mind."

Ephesians 3:20 KJV
"Now unto Him who is able to do exceeding abundantly above all that we can ask or think, according to the power that worketh in us."

Luke 10:19 KJV
"Behold, I give you power to tread over serpents and scorpions, and over all the power of the enemy: and nothing shall, by any means, hurt you."

The power given to us by God, as His children, gives us the ability to conquer obstacles, trials, and enemies. You are powerful because the God you serve is powerful.

Queen

Genesis 2:22 KJV
"And the rib, which the Lord God had taken from man, made he a woman, and brought her unto the man."

Proverbs 31:30 NIV
"Charm is deceptive, and beauty is fleeting, but a woman who fears the Lord is to be praised."

Proverbs 18:22 KJV
"Whosoever findeth a wife findeth a good thing, and obtaineth favor from the Lord."

A woman of God is a queen and a blessing from God.

Repent

Matthew 4:17 KJV
"From that time, Jesus began to preach and to say, 'Repent, for the kingdom of heaven is at hand.'"

Acts 3:19 NKJV
"Repent therefore, and be converted, that your sins may be blotted out, so that times of refreshing may come from the presence of the Lord."

Luke 15:10 NKJV
"Likewise, I say to you, there is joy in the presence of the angels of God over one sinner who repents."

Repentance is an act of confessing your sins to God and to those you've sinned against, and asking for their forgiveness. Change is the evidence of true repentance.

Restoration

Psalms 80:19 NKJV
"Restore us, O Lord God of hosts; Cause Your face to shine, And we shall be saved!"

I Kings 18:37 NKJV
"Hear me, O Lord, hear me, that this people may know that You are the Lord God, and that You have turned their hearts back to You again."

Ephesians 2:13 NKJV
"But now in Christ Jesus, you who once were far off have been brought near by the blood of Christ."

Restoration is the act of returning back. No matter what wrong doings or poor choices we make, God is always waiting for us to return back to Him.

Sacrifice

I Peter 2:5 NKJV
"You also, as living stones, are being built up a spiritual house, a holy priesthood, to offer up spiritual sacrifices acceptable to God through Jesus Christ."

Romans 12:1 NKJV
"I beseech you therefore, brethren, by the mercies of God, that you present your bodies a living sacrifice, holy, acceptable to God, which is your reasonable service."

Hebrews 13:16 NKJV
"But do not forget to do good and to share, for with such sacrifices God is well pleased."

Sacrifice is an act of surrendering to God and placing one's self and desires second place to God and others.

Thankfulness

I Thessalonians 5:18 NKJV
"In everything, give thanks; for this is the will of God in Christ Jesus for you."

Psalms 35:18 NKJV
"I will give You thanks in the great assembly; I will praise You among many people."

Psalms 107:1 NKJV
"Oh, give thanks to the Lord, for He is good! For His mercy endures forever."

Giving thanks to God shows how much you appreciate Him, and it also activates blessings.

Unbelief

Matthew 13:58 NKJV
"Now He did not do many mighty works there because of their unbelief."

Mark 9:24 NKJV
"Immediately, the father of the child cried out and said with tears, "Lord, I believe; help my unbelief!"

James 1:6 NKJV
"But let him ask in faith, with no doubting, for he who doubts is like a wave of the sea driven and tossed by the wind."

Unbelief is doubt, and is rooted in fear or lack of trust. It can hinder prayers and your relationship with God and others. Believe.

Victory

I Chronicles 29:11 NKJV
"Yours, O Lord, is the greatness, the power and the glory, the victory and the majesty; for all that is in heaven and in earth is Yours. Yours is the kingdom, O Lord, And You are exalted as head over all."

Philippians 4:13 NKJV
"I can do all things through Christ who strengthens me."

I Corinthians 15:57 NKJV
"But thanks be to God, who gives us the victory through our Lord Jesus Christ."

Victory is the ability to defeat or overcome. God has given you, His child, victory over all life's circumstances.

Wisdom

James 3:17 NKJV
"But the wisdom that is from above is first pure, then peaceable, gentle, willing to yield, full of mercy and good fruits, without partiality and without hypocrisy."

Proverbs 4:7 NKJV
"Wisdom is the principal thing; therefore, get wisdom. And in all your getting, get understanding."

James 1:5 NKJV
"If any of you lacks wisdom, let him ask of God, who gives to all liberally and without reproach, and it will be given to him."

Wisdom is determined by how accurately knowledge is applied. Christian wisdom is determined by how you accurately apply the word of God to your life.

Psalms 103:5 NKJV
"Who satisfies your mouth with good things, so that your youth is renewed like the eagle's."

Psalms 71:17 NKJV
"O God, You have taught me from my youth, and to this day I declare Your wondrous works."

I Timothy 4:12 NKJV
"Let no one despise your youth, but be an example to the believers in word, in conduct, in love, in spirit, in faith, in purity."

It is important to seek God in your youth.

Zeal

Isaiah 42:13 NKJV
"The Lord shall go forth like a mighty man. He shall stir up His zeal like a man of war. He shall cry out, yes, shout aloud. He shall prevail against His enemies."

II Kings 10:16 NKJV
"Then he said, 'Come with me, and see my zeal for the Lord.' So they had him ride in his chariot."

Philippians 1:20 NKJV
"According to my earnest expectation and hope that in nothing I shall be ashamed, but with all boldness, as always, so now also Christ will be magnified in my body, whether by life or by death."

To have zeal is to have great eagerness or energy for something. Have the zeal to share the gospel of Jesus Christ and to win souls.

God bless you world. This is Darryl G. Stanton, and I pray that you are having an awesome, wonderful, blessed morning.

I would like to invite you all on this journey with me. I did my first chemotherapy treatment on September 30, 2019, at the cancer center. My body received it well. I had to bring home the new chemo ball and machine, which will run for two days. It is really a miracle of God.

We want to thank you all for your prayers. We are praying for you and your family as well.

Hello world,

It is time for my journey with chemotherapy treatment number two, on Monday, October 28. I am blessed to be gaining weight and eating healthy, and to be able to continue to do what I have been called to do. The chemo treatments are going extremely well. Thank God.

Those of you who are on this journey with me and my queen, our family would like to say thank you for your prayers. I am doing great. Thanks.

Hello world,

This is Darryl G. Stanton. I pray that you are having an awesome, wonderful, blessed evening. Tomorrow is chemotherapy treatment number three. I will have the first round of chemo, and then come home with the chemo ball and machine. The chemo will run for two more days, which is Tuesday and Wednesday, and I will be done on Thursday at 11:00 a.m.

All is well in Jesus' name.

With God's love,

Darryl and Jana.

Hello world, and all who are on this journey with me and my queen.

Chemotherapy treatment number four is here, and I want to share with you all that I went to my first kidney doctor appointment yesterday, where he also read a report that showed that cancer was found in other areas of my body. He named the areas, but it doesn't matter. Why not? Because I believe the report of the Lord, and by his stripes I am healed. That report didn't move me because I have the victory already. Amen. Praise God. It's all for the glory of God.

Hello world,

This is Darryl. It is time for chemotherapy treatment number five. I pray that you all are having an awesome, wonderful, blessed day. I am blessed to be alive. I thank God for continuing to cover and protect me. Thank you all for your prayers.

With God's love,

Darryl and Jana.

Hello world,

This is Darryl. It is time for chemotherapy treatment number six, on Monday. I pray that you all are having an awesome, wonderful, blessed morning. I am blessed to be alive. I am grateful for life itself. Thank you all for your prayers. We are grateful for you all.

With God's love,

Darryl and Jana.

Hello world,

This is Darryl. I pray that you are having an awesome, wonderful, blessed morning. It's time for chemotherapy treatment number seven. I am grateful for my treatment. The cancer is shrinking. Thank God. I am doing very well with my chemo treatment. God is good and faithful to his word.

For those of you who are on this journey with me and my queen, thank you for your prayers. We are thankful to God for you all.

With God's love,

Darryl and Jana.

Hello world,

This is Darryl. I pray that you all are having an awesome, wonderful, blessed evening. It is time for chemotherapy treatment number eight. I thank God for my treatment because our God is using chemo to destroy the white cells, and that is a blessing.

For those of you that are on the journey with me and my queen, we ask that you keep praying for us. We are praying for you all as well.

With God's love,

Darryl and Jana.

Hello world,

This is Darryl. I pray that you all are having an awesome, wonderful, blessed evening. Chemotherapy treatment number nine went well. I had a meeting with a doctor today, and she told me that all my lab work was great, and that I am doing very well. I am still gaining weight, and I am grateful to our God for the miracles He is doing in my body.

I was able to witness and share God's love with some patients today. Amen. Praise God. It's all for the glory of God.

Hello world,

This is Darryl. I pray that you all are having an awesome, wonderful, blessed Sunday evening. On Monday morning I will have chemotherapy treatment number ten. Praise God.

God's will is being done, and I am feeling well. To God be the glory. Thank you all for your prayers. We couldn't have gotten to this point without you all.

With God's love,

Darryl and Jana.

Hello world,

This is Darryl. It's time for chemotherapy treatment number eleven this morning. Thank you all for your prayers. It's working, because I have no pain at all, and never had pain during my treatment. I know that is God's doing.

Praise God. He has protected me during this process, and we are praying for everyone that is dealing with any form of cancer, that our God will do the same for them as well. Please join your faith with me and my queen, and pray with us for all cancer patients.

Thank you all for all your prayers. We are grateful for you all.

With God's love,

Darryl and Jana.

Hello world,

This is Darryl. I pray that you all are having an awesome, wonderful, blessed evening. Tomorrow, it will be time for chemotherapy treatment number twelve. God has truly been good during this journey. I have no complaints. I am so blessed to be alive and doing well, by the mercy of God.

I am praying for other cancer patients on their journey, as we are believing in God for your miracle of healing as well.

My hair is growing back. I usually wear a bald head. I am looking forward to getting a nice haircut soon. Thank God. Thank you all for your prayers.

My weight has been going back and forth from 137 to 145. The cancer sometimes causes pain in my hip. That level of pain is a 1 and comes 1-3 times a month as of now.

Hello world,

This is Darryl. I would like to share with you all that the spirit of God told me to tell the people to fear not. God's perfect love casts out all fear.

Please be encouraged and know that our God is in control. Yes, this is a time to give our God the opportunity to show us how much He loves us.

My queen and I would like to issue a challenge to the world this morning. Our challenge is for you to give God thirty-one days of your life and see what He will do. God love us so much that he has an awesome, wonderful, blessed plan for your life.

With God's love,

Darryl and Jana.

Hello world,

This is Darryl. Chemotherapy treatment is going well this morning. Praise God. I have gained three more pounds, and my weight is now 153 pounds. I Thank God for your prayers.

Hello world,

This is Darryl. I just finished the final chemotherapy treatment, and it went extremely well. To God be the glory.

They will do another CT scan, and me and my queen believe that all the cancer is gone. My hair is growing back on my face and head, even though I wear a bald head. Anyway, it's a great sign that the cancer is shrinking fast. God is still doing miracles. Praise God. Amen.

We are grateful for you all covering us in prayers.

With God's love,

Darryl and Jana.

Hello world,

This is Darryl. I pray that you all are having an, awesome, wonderful, blessed morning. Me and my queen are excited about what our God is doing. God is showing the world that he is bigger than anything we are facing right now. He is bigger than any disease. God is good and true to his word. I feel wonderful this morning.

Praise God. It's all for the glory of God. Amen.

With God's love,

Darryl and Jana.

Hello world,

I would like to ask you all to keep in your prayers the book that God has asked me to write. Pray that God will use this tool to encourage people around the world to accomplish their goals, no matter what obstacles they may face.

You can begin again right now. Keep God first in your life, and watch what He will do.

With God's love,

Darryl.

2017, after colon cancer surgery. And months later, it turned into stage 4 colon cancer and spread to my liver.

2018, God healed me of Stage 4 colon cancer.

This book is dedicated to the most important people in my life.

Jana D. Stanton (My queen)
Celebrating our 26-year
anniversary in December 2022

Verna Stanton (My mother)
(1934-2018)

George Hackett (My father)
(1939-2021)

These are my business advisors and mentors,
as well as my new family.

CJ Malone

Victor (Phazz) Clark

Thank you all so much for your business advice and mentorship, and for becoming my new family.

With love,

Darryl

Pastor Mondoe and Lisa Davis

Afterword

I'll never forget the wave of emotion I experienced as my wife, Lisa, and I met Darryl and Jana for the first time. I felt as if I was being infused with a surge of inspiration, courage, and hope all at the same time. We were at the Gateway Church café at the North Fort Worth campus, between weekend services. I had just been hired on staff, and I was filled with hope and expectation regarding my new assignment to expand the Gospel of Jesus Christ. When I realized Darryl was going to be one of my new co-workers, I was overwhelmed with joy. I thought, *This is the type of person I want to spend my time with. He is so encouraging, inspiring, and uplifting.* I witnessed unyielding faith and encouragement that was seldom found in others.

Show me someone with unprecedented joy, and I will show you someone who has overcome unprecedented circumstances. In my experience, the people who have the most joy in life have likely gone through extremely challenging circumstances, and have overcome them. Little did I know, this theory would hold to be true as I spent time getting to know Darryl and Jana over the coming weeks, months, and years. I learned that he not only overcame insurmountable odds, but found a way to be an encouragement to everyone he was around, despite his challenges. I learned that Darryl was diagnosed with several types of cancer at several stages of his life. Not only is he alive and well, but he beat cancer and won every time.

If you've received a discouraging report, diagnosis, or bad news, this book is designed to give you the encouragement you need to persevere and break through. Darryl chose to stand on the word of God, and stand in faith, after going through numerous treatments, not being able to work, and facing severe discouragement James 1:2-8 AMP. ²Consider it nothing but joy, my brothers and sisters, whenever you fall into various trials. ³Be assured that the testing of your faith [through experience] produces endurance [leading to spiritual maturity, and inner peace]. ⁴And let endurance have its perfect result, *and* do a thorough work, so that you may be perfect and completely developed [in your faith], lacking in nothing.

⁵If any of you lacks wisdom [to guide him through a decision or circumstance], he is to ask of [our benevolent] God, who gives to everyone generously, and without rebuke or blame, and it will be given to him. ⁶But he must ask [for wisdom] in faith, without doubting [God's willingness to help]. For the one who doubts is like a billowing surge of the sea that is blown about and tossed by the wind. ⁷For such a person ought not to think or expect that he will receive anything [at all] from the Lord, ⁸being a double-minded man, unstable and restless in all his ways [in everything he thinks, feels, or decides].

Overcoming cancer several times was a transformational part of Darryl's life that led to him to write this book during such a difficult time around the world. With everything that is happening in our nation and around the world, it is easy to be discouraged. Darryl successfully overcame insurmountable odds, and lives to encourage you with what helped him overcome his circumstances.

Whether you believe it or not, there is an assault being launched against you every day, to steal your joy, peace, and courage John 10:10 AMP. ¹⁰The thief comes only in order to steal and kill and destroy. I came that they may have and enjoy life, and have it in abundance [to the full, till it overflows].

Discouragement is defined as: *to deprive of courage or confidence.* There are so many aspects of society that provide an overdose of discouragement on a daily basis. Whether you are dealing with a health crisis, financial crisis, relational crisis, or any other situation, discouragement is always readily available in overwhelming doses. On the other hand, *encouragement* is defined by Webster's dictionary as: *to inspire with courage, spirit, or hope.*

The word *encourage* is made up of two parts: *en–courage*, which literally means to put strength back into you. To do what frightens you in the face of pain or grief.

Satan came to take your confidence and discourage, while Jesus came to give life and put courage back into you so you can live the life He called you to live.

Every year, many organizations do a workplace survey to assess the health of their organization and the employees within it. I learned that, after assessing what employees wanted most, the Best Christian Workplaces Survey found that what people wanted more than more vacation time, higher salaries, and more perks was genuine encouragement from their boss and co-workers. They want to know their work matters, while receiving encouragement from the people they are co-laboring with.

With the work of your hands, I want you to be encouraged to know that things are not as bad as they seem, and may not be as good as they appear to be. Stay steady and keep your focus on leaving the world a better place than you found it by taking in a daily dose of encouragement.

The question is, not *if*, but *when* you go through hard times in life, how will you respond? It is not a matter of whether life will affect you in a negative way, but how you will choose to respond, which will determine your success or failure.

I'll never forget when Darryl asked me to consider the great honor of officiating his mother's celebration of life service after she passed away and went to be with the Lord. I had the privilege of visiting Darryl and his mother before she passed in the nursing home. He was by her side daily, until she passed away, and what impressed me most was how encouraging he was not only to me, but to the hospital staff and everyone he came in contact with. In the midst of pain, he found a way to encourage himself. He has compiled the scriptures, thoughts, and words that helped him overcome cancer several times and make it through losing his mother. Those scriptures, thoughts, and words have been compiled to help you find hope and encouragement to overcome the pain and obstacles in your life as well.

No matter where you are, and no matter what you are going through, Jesus died for you not only for you to have an eternal relationship with him, but to also find peace in the midst of every storm you will go through. Psalm 118:24 says, "This is the day that the Lord has made; let us rejoice and be glad in it." Be encouraged today. Find your joy again. You can't change your past, or determine the future, but you can be encouraged to open the gift of the present!

May God bless you as you take in this daily dose of encouragement!

Mondoe Davis
Gateway Church North Fort Worth
Campus Pastor

My name is Darryl G. Stanton. I would like to dedicate this new book to my queen and wife, Jana Stanton, and to the memory of my mother, Queen Verna Lee Stanton, and to my awesome father, King George Hackett. I thank God for the opportunity to share this book with the world. I pray that this book will bless you as much as it has blessed us.

I would like to share a little of my testimony with the world:

My journey began in 1973, when I was diagnosed at ten years old, with Crohn's disease. I endured this illness for many years, and God healed me. My prayer is that anyone that is dealing with any form of Cancer God will heal them as he has healed me. Please don't give up believing in your healing, because God is a healer. I am a witness to that.

In Jesus' name, amen. Praise God. It is all for the glory of God.

I was diagnosed with multiple myeloma (bone cancer) in 2012, and God healed me of that as well. In 2017, after getting through colon cancer surgery, months later it turned into stage 4 colon cancer that had spread to my liver. But God healed me in 2018. Praise God!

On September 18, 2019, I was diagnosed with stage 4 colon cancer again, and it had once again spread to my liver, as well as other areas of my body. But God healed me from the other cancers, and God will do it again.

Amen. Praise God. It's all for the glory of God.

Now I am blessed to bring forth a new book in 2021. I am taking my life back, in Jesus' name.

With God's love,

Darryl.

The Salvation Prayer

God bless you, world. This is Darry. I pray you are having an awesome, wonderful, blessed day.

I would like to give those who are interested, the opportunity to receive Jesus Christ as their Lord and Savior. This is a wonderful season to receive Jesus Christ, because Jesus is the reason for the season. Repeat this prayer after me:

> *Dear Jesus, I ask you to forgive me for my sins. I believe that you died and rose from the dead to save me from my sins. Here I am right now, with an open heart to you, asking you to come into my heart and my life, and be my personal Lord and Savior. I receive you now. Amen. Praise God.*

Welcome to the family of God. I encourage you to get connected to a church where the love of God is present, and they are teaching the word from the Bible. You will begin to grow in your relationship with God the Father, God the Son, God the Holy Spirit, and in the word of God. God loves you and has and awesome plan for your life.

Send your testimonies, salvation testimonies, and your thirty-one-day challenge testimonies to: EncouragingWords.dgs@gmail.com

With God's love,

Darryl.

www.ingramcontent.com/pod-product-compliance
Lightning Source LLC
Chambersburg PA
CBHW050044080526
44586CB00014B/1456